Artists in Profile

EXPRESSIONISTS

Merilyn Holme & Bridget McKenzie

www.heinemann.co.uk/library
Visit our website to find out more information about **Heinemann Library** books.

To order:
 Phone 44 (0) 1865 888066
 Send a fax to 44 (0) 1865 314091
 Visit the Heinemann Bookshop at www.heinemann.co.uk/library to browse our catalogue and order online.

First published in Great Britain by Heinemann Library, Halley Court, Jordan Hill, Oxford OX2 8EJ, a division of Reed Educational and Professional Publishing Ltd. Heinemann is a registered trademark of Reed Educational & Professional Publishing Limited.

OXFORD MELBOURNE AUCKLAND JOHANNESBURG BLANTYRE
GABORONE IBADAN PORTSMOUTH NH (USA) CHICAGO

Designed by Tinstar Design (www.tinstar.co.uk)
Originated by Ambassador Litho Ltd
Printed by South China Printing Company, Hong Kong / China

ISBN 0 431 11643 1
06 05 04 03 02
10 9 8 7 6 5 4 3 2 1

British Library Cataloguing in Publication Data
McKenzie, Bridget
  Expressionists. - (Artists in profile)
  1.Expressionism (Art) - Juvenile literature
  I.Title II.Holmes, Merilyn

Acknowledgements
The Publishers would like to thank the following for permission to reproduce photographs:
AKG London pp17, 27, 33, 38, 47, 50; AKG London/©DACS 2002 p35; Busch-Reisinger Museum, Cambridge (Mass.)/AKG London/©DACS 2002 p10; E. Lessing/AKG London p31; E. Lessing/SMPK Nationalgalerie, Berlin/AKG London/©DACS 2002 p9; Germanisches Nationalmuseum, Nurnberg p20; Historisches Museum der Stadt, Vienna, Austria/Bridgeman Art Library p53; Menard Art Museum, Aichi (Japan)/AKG London/©DACS 2002 p15; Munch Museum, Oslo p43; Museum Folkwang, Essen p40; Museum Ludwig, Cologne/AKG London p22; Neue Pinakothek Munich/Artothek p37; Nolde - Stiftung Seebull p49; Paul Klee Foundation, Bern, Switzerland/Bridgeman Art Library/©DACS 2002 p4; Paul Klee stiftung kunstmuseum, Bern©DACS 2002 p25; Peggy Guggenheim Collection, Venice/Cameraphoto/AKG London/©DACS 2002 p54; Photo Scala, Florence©DACS 2002 p45; Sprengel Museum, Hannover p51; Stadt Galerie im Lenbachhaus, Munich/AKG London p39; Stedelijk Van Abbe Museum, Eindhoven/AKG London/©DACS 2002 p29; Tate, London 2002/©DACS 2002 pp7, 12, 18; Westfalisches Landesmuseum, Munster/AKG London p36.

Cover photograph ©Nolde-Stiftung Seebull/AKG.

Our thanks to Richard Stemp for his help in the preparation of this book.

Every effort has been made to contact copyright holders of any material reproduced in this book. Any omissions will be rectified in subsequent printings if notice is given to the Publisher.

Contents

Words appearing in the text in bold, **like this**, are explained in the glossary.

What is Expressionism?

Expressionism is an art movement that produced a wealth of wonderful works of art, and the lives of the artists who created them were no less colourful and exciting. The word 'expressionism' can be used to describe art from different times and places, but most of the Expressionist artists in this book were part of a movement that took place in Germany from 1905 to 1920. Other artists have been included because they influenced those German Expressionist artists or they shared some of their beliefs. Those beliefs were that art should try to change society, to make it less **conservative**. It should express the energy of nature – following in the footsteps of Vincent van Gogh – and personal feeling rather than simply representing nature. It should feel 'uncomfortable', which means it should challenge the traditional ways of looking at the world. This differed from the opinion of Henri Matisse who believed that art should be 'comfortable'. Expressionist art should be inspired by folk art, and the art of what were then called '**primitive**' peoples, for example from Africa.

Plan einer Garten-Architektur, by Paul Klee (1920)
The aim of the Expressionists was to express personal feeling about what they were painting rather than representing it exactly as it was.

4

It should have strong colours and shapes, be relatively direct, untutored and unplanned and should still contain recognizable things, but not be realistic. The lines could be distorted, and the colours could be strengthened or changed as in the art movement that began in 1905 called **Fauvism**.

Expressionism was more than a style in painting. It could be found in theatre and cinema, literature and architecture. It was a sharing of ideas and experiences across all these media. The life stories of the Expressionist artists show just how much they had in common. Many began by studying **applied art**, such as furniture design, often to please their parents. Although they later made more personal art, they continued to make use of those technical skills. Both art critics and the public received this new movement with derision and outrage. Expressionist artists were trying to shock by challenging the traditional, conservative views held by many people. Gradually, however, it became accepted and even admired.

All the Expressionists were affected by World War I (1914–18). Some fled from Germany and spent the war years in exile. Some never returned to their homeland. Most served in the war and some were killed. At first some of them hoped a war would change society for the better but they were soon disillusioned when they saw the destruction and suffering that it caused. In the years after the war, many Expressionist artists revealed the horrors they experienced in their work.

After World War I Expressionism became very fashionable in Germany, where art was allowed to flourish. This freedom ended in 1933 when Hitler declared all Expressionists were '**degenerate**'. This led to them being sacked from their jobs or forced to leave Germany. In 1937 the Nazis took thousands of art works from German museums and put them in an enormous exhibition called the Degenerate Art Exhibition, to show how bad and **decadent** this art was. It presented a view of the world that went against their political and cultural ambitions to rid Germany of all inferior races.

Vincent van Gogh 1853–90

The German Expressionists and the French Fauvists were very influenced by the paintings of Vincent van Gogh, who presented a highly personal view of nature. He used vivid colours and exaggerated, swirling brushstrokes to give a sense of energy and movement to everything he portrayed. He said, 'Instead of trying to reproduce exactly what I have before my eyes, I use colour more arbitrarily [in an unplanned way] so as to express myself more forcibly.' This Dutch artist moved to Arles in the South of France in 1888, where he painted over two hundred pictures in two years. He was suffering from bouts of insanity at this time, however, which led to him committing suicide in 1890.

Fauvism and Matisse

An exhibition in 1905 at the **Salon** d'Automne in Paris kicked off the first **avant-garde** art movement of the 20th century. The colours of the paintings by Matisse, Derain and Vlaminck that were shown in this exhibition were more vivid and unrealistic than had ever been seen before. The artists were labelled *'fauves'* or 'wild beasts', and were a big influence on the German Expressionists.

Henri Matisse (1869–1954) was one of the **Fauvists**. He wrote, 'What I dream of is an art of balance, of purity and serenity ... like a comforting influence, a mental balm – something like a good armchair.' This belief that art should be comfortable was where he differed from the Expressionists, who believed that art should express one's true feelings, however ugly and violent they may sometimes be.

The Nazis disliked Expressionist artists because many lived in an unconventional, **bohemian** way. They did not tend to settle in their home towns because they needed to search for like-minded artists and new ideas for their art. They travelled outside their countries to see other artists' work, as good colour reproductions were not available. In particular, they wanted to visit France to see art by van Gogh, Derain, Matisse and Delaunay, whom they especially admired. They were also keen to meet artists and thinkers from other countries. A large number taught in art schools and were quite intellectual thinkers and writers. Expressionism was about more than personal emotions. Most were active members of artist groups, so that they could display their art together and make public, sometimes shocking, statements about their beliefs.

Although a great deal was shared, above all Expressionism was about the strength of the individual. Through their art the Expressionists stated that emotions matter and should not be repressed, that our feelings distort our vision, making us all see the world in unique ways.

Die Brücke

Brücke means 'bridge'. This choice of name suggests that this group of artists wanted to forge a path to the future. They also wanted to make a bridge between fine art and design. They were driven by the ideas of Ernst Kirchner, who with Fritz Bleyl, Erich Heckel and Karl Schmidt-Rottluff formed the group in 1905 in Dresden. At the time they were all architecture students interested in painting. They believed that all artists should feel free to express themselves in a way that comes naturally to them, unrestricted by traditional, established values and styles.

Male Head, by Karl Schmidt-Rottluff (1917)
Schmidt-Rottluff, a former architecture student, was a founding member of Die Brücke. It was he who introduced Emil Nolde to the group.

A statement of 1906 says, 'We believe in development and in a generation of people who are both creative and appreciative; we call together all young people, and – as young people who bear the future – we want to acquire freedom for our hands and lives, against the well-established older forces.'

Common themes of *Die Brücke* paintings are nude people and unspoiled nature. But their painting style, compared to *Der Blaue Reiter* artists, could be quite harsh, with angular figures, colours that combined clashing, acid brights with moody darks, and nervous brushstrokes. Some might say that their style was so rough because they had not been trained to paint, others that it was the result of the direct expression of emotion. As well as painting, they made a lot of woodcut prints, because they thought this old German art form was well suited to the expression of feelings with its strong black and white contrasts. They made many copies of their prints so that as many people as possible could see and own their work.

Der Blaue Reiter

Der Blaue Reiter is German for 'The Blue Rider'. It was not the name of a fixed group of artists, but of a magazine or 'almanac' containing writings about art, music and theatre. It was illustrated with folk, medieval and Egyptian art, and drawings by children and many **Fauve** and Expressionist artists. Wassily Kandinsky produced this almanac in 1912 with Paul Klee, Franz Marc, August Macke, Gabriele Münter and Alexei von Jawlensky. All the artists involved in *Der Blaue Reiter* were located in or near Munich and had an interest in freeing the picture from the object. They believed that art did not have to mirror actual appearances. Their art was very colourful and was becoming quite **abstract**, especially in Kandinsky's case. It was more attractively decorative than work by the *Die Brücke* artists. They were influenced by both German and Russian folk art. They liked its stories and its simple woodcut styles and flat compositions.

The Bauhaus

The Bauhaus was a school of design, and a 'thinktank' for **modernism**. It was set up in 1919 by Walter Gropius. Like the *Brücke* artists he wanted to mix fine art with design, so many of the teachers were painters, including Kandinsky and Klee. They could give the architecture and design students a more sensitive awareness of colour and form. The typical Bauhaus design style is very geometrical and simple and not very 'Expressionist'. The school moved city three times and was finally closed by the Nazis in 1933.

■ *The Almanac, Der Blaue Reiter,* Wassily Kandinsky (1912)
The almanac was edited by Kandinsky and Marc and included contributions by both Expressionist and Fauvist artists. In 1930 Kandinsky wrote: 'We invented the name 'Der Blaue Reiter' while sitting at a coffee table in the garden in Sindelsdorf; we both loved blue, Marc liked horses, I riders. So the name came by itself.'

Max Beckmann 1884–1950

- Born 12 February 1884 in Leipzig, in the centre of Germany.
- Died 27 December 1950 from a heart attack while walking in Central Park, New York.

Key works

The Self-portrait with a Red Scarf, 1917
The Night, 1918–19
The Synagogue, 1919
Carnival, 1920
Before the Masked Ball, 1922
Departure, 1932–5

Self-portrait with Dinner-suit, by Max Beckmann (1927) 'What I want to show in my work is the idea which hides itself behind so-called reality. I am seeking for the bridge which leads from the visible to the invisible...' (Max Beckmann speaking of his work in 1938).

Max Beckmann was born in 1884, the third child of a wholesale flour merchant. The family lived in Leipzig until Beckmann's father died in 1894, when they moved to Braunschweig (Brunswick). Here, Beckmann went to school. He started to draw at the age of five and neglected his schoolwork in favour of this activity. Finally, aged only fifteen, he was allowed by his mother to leave school and go to the Weimar Academy of Art. He stayed for three years and gained a solid training in painting people. In 1903 he visited Paris. In 1904, he won a prize to study for six months in Florence, Italy, where he could see all the early religious art he wanted. He was interested in how pictures could tell stories in passionate but clear ways. In 1905, he moved to Berlin which was the cultural and administrative centre of Germany.

Beckmann's first paintings reflected his liking of the Impressionist and Post-Impressionist paintings he had seen in Paris. In 1906 he was awarded a prize for his picture *Young Men by the Sea* by the German Artists' League at Weimar. That same year he joined a group of artists called the Berlin **Secession** and he also got married to Minna Tube, a fellow artist whom he had met at the Weimar Academy. He turned again to early French and Dutch painting and the subjects he chose for his pictures were mostly biblical and mythical scenes.

However, this changed after World War I. He had volunteered for the medical corps, which meant that he had to help badly wounded soldiers. This experience led to a mental breakdown only a year later in 1915 and he was invalided out of the army to a hospital in Frankfurt.

Otto Dix 1891–1969

Otto Dix, Beckmann and George Grosz were the main artists of the '**New Objectivity**' movement of the 1920s, which was a reaction against Expressionism. In 1927 Dix said, 'For me the object comes first, and it is the object that orients [directs] form.' He was also involved in the **Dada** movement. This developed in Europe as a reaction to the destruction of World War I and encouraged the use of chance happenings and the absurd in the making of art. As a professor at the Dresden Academy of Art he did not hide his political beliefs so, like Beckmann, he lost his job when the Nazis came to power and was labelled a '**degenerate**'. In 1939 he was even sent to prison for plotting to kill Hitler.

Beckmann carried on painting in hospital for the next two years, trying to make sense of the horrors he had seen. He had gone from painting biblical scenes to scenes showing human cruelty and torture. Into his picture spaces he crowded a lot of figures and objects, which twist and jut out at us, giving a strange, claustrophobic feeling. It is this anxiety that makes him close to Expressionism. At a time when other Expressionists were exploring **abstraction**, he decided to be a **history painter**, but not to record official history for the ruling powers. Instead he wanted to show the unofficial history, the everyday suffering in European cities.

■ *Carnival*, by Max
Beckmann (1920)
*Beckmann's work
changed after his
experiences during
World War I. He
started to produce
harsh, disjointed
paintings that
differed from his
earlier biblical
scenes.*

He made large pictures and often used the shapes of religious altarpieces, for example the three panels of a **triptych**, so that they were noticed and taken seriously. He became one of Germany's foremost painters, part of the movement called '**New Objectivity**'.

In 1925, when he was 41 years old, Beckmann was appointed to teach at an art college in Frankfurt. Also in 1925 he divorced his wife Minna and married Mathilde von Kaulbach, who featured in many of his important paintings. In 1929 he was promoted to professor, and over the next four years had several major exhibitions and awards for his artistic achievements. In 1933 the Nazis came to power and because his art was so political, they sacked him from his professorship. Along with that of the other Expressionists, they considered his work to be socially and morally corrupt and labelled him '**degenerate**'. He moved then to Berlin to attract less attention. In 1937, the Nazis confiscated 590 of his paintings from German museums. He became afraid for his safety and fled to Holland with his wife. Perhaps to express his anger, he wrote an article called 'My Theory of Painting', which is more about politics than it is about painting. Holland was not an easy place to live either, as it suffered **German occupation** and poverty during World War II. After the war was over he was able to emigrate to the USA in 1947, where he taught in Washington and New York. By this time he was widely accepted as one of the major forces in 20th-century art. He continued to paint until his death in New York in 1950.

George Grosz 1893–1959

Grosz was another member of the 'New Objectivity' movement. Although he believed in a 'new objectivity' he was also interested in an art that did not make sense. He helped set up the Club **Dada** in Berlin, editing its magazine and organizing a Dada fair. Like Dix he was very critical of the idea of military power and although he had fought in World War I, he was not at all a keen volunteer. Twice he had been dismissed as unfit for service and he was put on trial for attacking an officer. To show his disgust for his German nationality he and a friend, John Heartfield (Helmut Herzfeld), changed their names to English spellings. They sent each other postcards with small collages that hid criticisms of Germany. In 1931 he moved to New York to be a lecturer and stayed there to escape the Nazis, who labelled him 'degenerate'. In 1959 he returned to West Berlin, saying 'My American dream turned out to be a soap bubble' (he had failed to make much of a name for himself in the USA as an artist). He died in Berlin falling down some stairs.

James Ensor 1860–1949

> - Born on 13 April 1860 in Ostend, a port and fishing village on the Belgian coast.
> - He died in 1949 in Ostend.
>
> ## Key works
> *Woman Eating Oysters*, 1882
> *The Entry of Christ into Brussels*, 1888
> *Skeletons Warming Themselves*, 1889

James Ensor made some paintings before 1900 that showed signs of Expressionism, well before the Expressionist movement began. His work made a big impression on Paul Klee, who owned an etching by him.

Ensor's father was English and his mother was Belgian. He had a younger sister, Mariette. Their parents kept a souvenir shop, where the talented and imaginative boy grew up in a virtual treasure store of grotesque masks, puppets and exotic and colourful bric-à-brac. The false faces of these masks and puppets appear in many of his paintings. However, Ensor's imagination was really fired by two of the most famous Belgian artists of all time, Hieronymus Bosch (c.1450–1516) and Pieter Bruegel the Elder (1525–69). He would have seen copies of their gruesome and comic depictions of monsters and people oddly transformed.

Ensor spent three years studying at the Brussels Academy, from 1877 to 1880. His earliest mature paintings were largely of interior scenes and landscapes in sombre colours. This style was a strong contrast to the light, bright work of the Impressionists who were so fashionable at the time. The years 1880–1900 were his most productive and by the age of 22 he had exhibited in the Brussels **Salon** and the prestigious Paris Salon.

Ensor was disgusted by the vanity and vulgarity that he witnessed in Ostend's holiday crowds and began to use them for his subject matter. The following year his painting called *Woman Eating Oysters* was refused by the Salons, the first of many considered too controversial for public taste. He had by now begun to re-introduce the masks and skeletons of his early work and used them to criticize the behaviour of the society in which he lived. His *Cathedral* shows an unruly, masked crowd acting out a **parody** of a religious festival. It is a criticism of the people's insincerity rather than of the Church.

In 1883 the **Twenty Group** was formed and Ensor exhibited at their first salon in 1884. His influence in the group waned with the increasing popularity of French art and he was expelled from the group in 1889 after the public outrage at his painting *The Entry of Christ into Brussels*.

Ensor was an isolated, often unhappy figure but an extremely original artist. He continued to paint subjects that criticized the state, the Church and the king, but nevertheless in 1929 the King of the Belgians made him a baron. He had by then been accepted as an artist of international importance and is today regarded as one of the founders of Expressionism. He enjoyed his last 20 years in Ostend being surrounded by young, admiring writers and artists. He died in 1949.

▌▌ *Self-portrait with masks*, by James Ensor (1899)
Ensor's early influences were reflected in his paintings of hideous, deformed masks and pictures overcrowded with people.

Wassily Kandinsky 1866–1944

- Born on 4 December 1866 in Moscow.
- Died 13 December 1944 at Neuilly-sur-Seine, near Paris, France.

Key works
Cossacks, 1910-11
Improvisation on No. 19, 1911
With a Black Arc, 1912
Dreamy Improvisation, 1913

Kandinsky was 30 before he began to study art, but he still had a long and successful career as an artist. He is important because he made some of the first experiments in **abstraction**.

Wassily Kandinsky was born in 1866 into a wealthy Russian family. His father was in charge of a tea company in Moscow. He went to nursery school in Florence, Italy but when his father's health got worse in 1871, the family moved back to Odessa, Russia. Shortly afterwards, Kandinsky's parents divorced and he was brought up by his aunt.

He had a very cultured upbringing. His parents were very musical and Kandinsky himself played the piano and cello from an early age. His love of colour and shape was influenced by watercolours that he was given by his aunt and he was encouraged to draw and paint in his spare time by both his aunt and his father. While he did take extra lessons in art and music at high school, he did not think of either subject as a possible career.

He began adult life studying economics and law from 1886 to 1892 at Moscow University. In his final university year he married his cousin, Ania Tchimiakin, and went on to work as a lecturer of law at Moscow University. Later he managed an art-printing factory and was then offered a lectureship at the University of Tartu in Estonia, which he refused. Compared to art though, his career seemed dull and heavy. He finally made his decision to give it up when he saw an exhibition featuring the Impressionist artist, Monet. Kandinsky was moved by a painting of a haystack. It showed him that art could have a deep effect just through its form. Kandinsky had not even realised until he read the catalogue that the picture was of a haystack.

■■■ *Wassily Kandinsky at his desk in the flat in Munich, June 1913.*

In 1896 he moved to Munich, a centre of artistic activity, to study art under the Slovenian realist artist, Anton Azbe. However, he was mature and ambitious – he wanted to learn as much as he could as quickly as possible. He was frustrated by Azbe's emphasis on painting nude models, so he spent a year working from home and out of doors, exploring colour. He wanted to be at the Munich Academy of Art, where everybody else tried to be, in the renowned teacher Franz von Stuck's drawing class. After two attempts, he was accepted in 1900. Although he felt he learned much from von Stuck himself, he found the whole atmosphere of the Academy stifling, saying it was 'the most certain means to kill off childhood genius'.

In 1901 Kandinsky left the Academy and co-founded the Phalanx group of artists, who ran an art school and put on exhibitions until 1904. One of these, in 1903, showed sixteen canvases by Monet. Kandinsky was making woodcut

▌▐ *Cossacks*, by Wassily Kandinsky (1910–11)
Kandinsky's Expressionist phase included paintings, such as Cossacks, which illustrated his love of primary colours. He thought that pure colours could powerfully influence people to the extent that the subject of the painting was of little importance.

prints, and designing clothing and posters in the **Jugendstil** fashion. His paintings then were decorative landscapes with a 'folk tale' atmosphere. He was very successful, winning prizes and exhibiting all over Europe.

Kandinsky's marriage to Ania had suffered when they left Russia and they finally separated in 1903. In 1902 he had met the woman who was to be his second partner, the painter Gabriele Münter. Over the next six years he travelled, often with her, to Italy, Holland, France, Switzerland, Tunisia and Russia. He returned to live in Munich in 1908. In the summer, he and Gabriele visited Murnau in the Bavarian countryside, which they found restful and inspiring, so the next year Gabriele bought a house there. It became her permanent home and Kandinsky visited regularly. Their friends Marianne von Werefkin and Alexei von Jawlensky, also artists, lived and painted there with them. Kandinsky's colours become more primary and his shapes stronger. One day he saw one of his paintings lying on its side looking blurred and beautiful in the half-light, and this spurred him to work towards **abstraction** (which he achieved by 1913).

In 1910 Kandinsky made friends with Franz Marc, an artist who had been one of the few people to express admiration for Kandinsky's new work. A year later they formed an editorial team called *Der Blaue Reiter* (see page 8) and published an almanac of the same name. Kandinsky published his first book *Concerning the Spiritual in Art* in 1912, about his theories that shape and colour could express **spiritual** meanings. It was a great success.

Kandinsky returned to Russia in 1914 because of World War I. He was persecuted because of his nationality. In 1916 he separated from Münter. He was very well connected in Russia because of his family, so after the Revolution in 1917 he had a series of high-level government jobs to develop culture. He was professor of the State Art Workshops and then in 1921 he co-founded the Moscow Academy of Arts. However, he disagreed with the main idea in Russia that industrial design was more important than fine art, so he went back to Germany.

Kandinsky taught at the Bauhaus in Weimar and Dresden from 1922 to 1933 (see page 8). In 1924 he formed the Blue Four artists' group with von Jawlensky, Klee and Lyonel Feininger. By then, Kandinsky had left his Expressionist phase and was painting in a purely abstract manner. In 1933 when the Nazis came to power and the Bauhaus was shut down, he left Germany to live in Neuilly-sur-Seine, near Paris, where he died in 1944.

Ernst Ludwig Kirchner 1880–1938

- Born 6 May 1880 in Aschaffenburg, near Dresden, Bavaria.
- Died 15 June 1938 near Davos, Switzerland.

Key works

Street, Berlin, 1913
Five Women in the Street, 1913
The Drinker (Self-portrait), 1915
Self-portrait as a Soldier, 1915

The Drinker (Self-portrait), by Ernst Kirchner (1915)
Kirchner suffered a mental and physical breakdown as a result of World War I. He later said he painted The Drinker *in Berlin 'while screaming military convoys were passing beneath my window day and night'.*

Kirchner was the brains behind the artists' group *Die Brücke*. He was a handsome man and a natural leader, but his personality was stormy. This caused some lost friendships and eventually, led to his suicide. He was a workaholic, producing thousands of paintings, prints and designs in his lifetime.

Ernst Ludwig Kirchner was born in 1880 in Germany to Maria Elise and Ernst Kirchner. He had two younger brothers, Hans Walter and Ulrich. Kirchner went to grammar school in Chemnitz, where two of his younger fellow pupils were Erich Heckel and Karl Schmidt-Rottluff. Kirchner showed an early talent in art which his parents praised and encouraged from the start. However, they opposed his wish to make art his career. Following his father's wishes, he studied architecture at the Technical School in Dresden from 1901 to 1903. The year 1903–4 was a significant time for Kirchner, when he attended an experimental art school in Munich and saw many exhibitions of French art. While in Munich he made a trip to nearby Nuremberg. Here he saw the work of the 15th-century artist, Albrecht Dürer – one of the greatest printmakers in art history. Kirchner was so inspired by Dürer's prints that he decided he wanted to become a painter. However, he needed to gain his degree so he returned to the Technical School in Dresden and graduated in architecture in 1905. It was there that he made friends with Fritz Bleyl, and later Erich Heckel and Karl Schmidt-Rottluff. The four became close when they discovered they all had more of an interest in fine art than architecture.

Erich Heckel 1883–1970 and Karl Schmidt-Rottluff 1884–1976

Heckel and Schmidt-Rottluff were two important founding members of *Die Brücke*. They went to the same school as Kirchner in Chemnitz but they were four years younger than Kirchner so they did not know him. It was not until Heckel went to Dresden in 1904 to study architecture that he became friends with Kirchner. Later Schmidt-Rottluff came to Dresden, also to study architecture, but he left the course after only two terms.

Heckel was enthusiastic and self-confident and it was his energy that kept the group together. It was also Heckel's studio, in an old butcher's shop, that the group worked in. However, it was Schmidt-Rottluff that invented the name 'Die Brücke'. Schmidt-Rottluff was less keen than Kirchner and Heckel to work communally in the same studios or on their trips to the lakes. Many of his paintings from the time are landscapes with no figures, some painted on the bracing North Sea coast or in Norway. You can see the connection with Emil Nolde, whom Schmidt-Rottluff introduced to the group. In 1914 he turned to painting figures, often sad-looking women to express the gloom of war coming. He also began making wooden figures inspired by African and Pacific sculptures. He served in the war from 1915 to 1918.

On 7 June 1905 Kirchner and his three friends founded *Die Brücke* and he wrote their **manifesto**. In 1908 they exhibited with the **Fauvists** and Kirchner's paintings became brighter and bolder like theirs. The exhibition was well received by the public, but Kirchner's parents were dismayed at their son's choice of career. They continued to disapprove in the years to come, although they helped out on the occasions when Kirchner was forced to ask them for money.

■ *A Group of Artists*, by Ernst Kirchner (1926)

Painted some time after the break up of Die Brücke, *Kirchner wanted to portray the friendship that had at first existed between the artists. It is noticeable though that Heckel is painted between the figures of Kirchner and Schmidt-Rottluff, the two most opposite members of* Die Brücke.

It was mainly Kirchner's idea that the group should spend summers out of Dresden to paint and live closer to nature. People's relationship to the natural world was an important influence to the members of *Die Brücke*. In 1908 Kirchner visited the Isle of Fehmarn in the Baltic Sea with his girlfriend Emmy Frisch and her brother. The bleakness of the sea made a strong impact on him. In the summers of 1909, 1910 and 1911 he and the group went often to the Moritzburg lakes to paint, taking other friends and models. Kirchner's romantic view of nature was replaced by an excitement for the city when in 1911 he moved from Dresden to Berlin. He wanted to show the tough and uncompromising nature of the city life he was surrounded by so his style changed to become less decorative and exotic and more gritty and sharp. For example, he now painted prostitutes and street scenes in which people merge with buildings. This perhaps reflects his state of mind in that he felt alone and unstable in Berlin, less close to his *Die Brücke* friends. He met Erna Schilling, who was to become his lifelong partner.

Kirchner published a history of *Die Brücke* in 1913 and this caused its break-up. His version of the story was that he had generated all the new ideas and the others had copied him. The others said he had been too dominating. Later he tried to say that the *Die Brücke* phase of his life was not important for his development. When World War I began he signed up for military service but described himself as an 'involuntary volunteer'. It did not suit him and only a year later he was discharged from the army, unable to cope with army life. In 1916 he wrote about the horrors that he had experienced during the war: 'The heaviest burden of all is the pressure of war and the increasing superficiality [shallowness]. It gives me incessantly the impression of a bloody carnival. I feel as though ... everything is topsy-turvy.' He suffered a mental breakdown and spent three years until 1918 recovering in hospitals. He believed that if he got well he would be made to fight again, so he resisted the healing process, growing dependent on sleeping pills, morphine and alcohol. He did, however, continue to paint and make woodcuts of the hospitals he was kept in.

His friends encouraged him to live in a healthier place than a German city so in 1918, accompanied by a nurse, he rented a farm near Davos in Switzerland. His partner Erna remained in Berlin to look after his studio. In Davos, surrounded by local farmers, he rediscovered the community spirit he had been searching for and he returned to natural themes in his paintings. He described his feeling for the landscape there in 1919: 'There was such a wonderful setting of the moon this morning, the yellow moon against little pink clouds, and the mountains a pure deep blue.' A few years later he moved to Wildboden in Switzerland and continued to paint. He had some major exhibitions in Switzerland. However, this success and the peace of his living situation were no defence against the Nazis. In 1937 they labelled him a '**degenerate**' and confiscated 639 of his works from museums in Germany, selling some abroad and destroying others. He tried to make his position safer by taking out Swiss citizenship for himself and Erna, but he became more and more depressed until he committed suicide in 1938.

Paul Klee 1879–1940

- Born on 18 December 1879 at Munchenbuchsee, near Berne, Switzerland.
- Died 29 June 1940 at Muralto-Locarno, Switzerland.

Key works

In the Houses of St Germain (Tunis), 1914
Zoo, 1918
Senecio, 1922
Carnival in the Mountains, 1924

Paul Klee is a unique and major artist, who produced about 8000 works of art. His work is so imaginative and delicate it is unlike the other Expressionists. It is perhaps more Surrealist than Expressionist. However, he was happy to work under the banner of 'Expressionism' because he wanted to find ways to 'make visible what has been perceived in secret'. This means he sought to express the feelings created in him by the world he saw around him rather than make an exact copy of them.

Paul Klee was born on 18 December 1879 in Switzerland. His mother, Ida Maria, was Swiss and his father Hans, was German. They were both musicians, although his father worked as a teacher. Paul inherited his father's sense of humour and was a talented violionist. He had a sister, Mathilde. Klee also had another special talent – he was ambidextrous and drew with his left hand and wrote with his right. As a schoolboy, Klee was popular because of his wit. He drew constantly, even throughout lessons, common subjects for his drawings being plants, cats, birds and fish. He did well only in music, poetry and art at school, so it was obvious that he was going to be an artist of some sort. Like Kandinsky, who came from Russia to study in Munich, Klee wanted to leave his homeland of Switzerland to study in the city where experimental artists were gathering. At the age of nineteen he started at Knirr's private art college. It was around this time that he first met his future wife, pianist, Lily Stumpf. In 1900, the same year as Kandinsky, he got a place in Franz von Stuck's class at the Academy of Fine Art. Here he struggled with colour and did not receive much help from von Stuck, who even suggested he should stop painting and become a sculptor instead. However, he did learn a great deal in 1901 by travelling round Italy to see art with his friend, the sculptor Hermann Haller. In Italy he was especially amazed by Leonardo da Vinci.

Because Klee was not earning money as an artist he went home to Berne in 1902, where he could play the violin in an orchestra while he developed his art. A trip to Paris in 1905 opened his eyes to modern French art but he said he had nothing to learn from it. Although his technique was steadily improving, he was still struggling to express himself in his paintings in the way that he wished. Some pictures he did exhibit at this time were criticized for their 'mad anatomy' – the forms were considered grotesque and misshapen. In 1906 he married Lily Stumpf and they settled in Munich, in a small flat. Lily gave piano lessons while Paul continued with his art. In 1907 they had a son, Felix. Paul, still the unknown artist, acted as 'house-husband' while Lily earned money with her teaching.

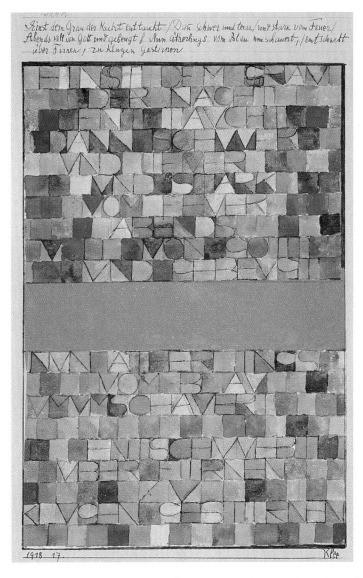

Einst dem Grau de Nacht entaucht (Once Emerged from the Grey of Night), by Paul Klee (1918)
Klee often used letters and numbers in his work to try to link dreams and reality.

In 1908 Klee saw two van Gogh exhibitions and was stunned by the expression of Van Gogh's emotion in his paintings. However, Klee did not feel he had that level of tragic passion in himself to put into his work. Klee was affected in the same way by James Ensor, a sample of whose work he was sent by a friend from Berne. A year later, in 1909, he saw a Cézanne exhibition for the first time and said, 'He is my teacher par excellence, much more so than van Gogh', perhaps because Cézanne's paintings are so carefully constructed and are less a show of emotions.

In 1909 Klee's pictures came more from his imagination and dreams, in a process that he called 'psychic improvisation'. He still liked to draw and paint from nature, but more and more he wished to express the feelings that his observations of natural objects inspired in him, rather than represent the objects themselves.

In 1910 Klee had some success with an exhibition that toured Switzerland and Munich, and in 1911 he met August Macke, who introduced him to Kandinsky. He also made friends with Franz Marc. He took part in the second exhibition of *Der Blaue Reiter*. These artists were all interested in the use of colour and greatly influenced Klee. He began to study pure colour – not as it appears in nature but the paintbox. They also introduced him to the work of the artist Robert Delaunay, whom he met in Paris in 1912. Klee was strongly influenced by Delaunay and he translated his writings about windows and light for publication in German.

In 1914 Klee made a happy visit to Tunis in North Africa with Macke. He said then, 'Colour has got me ... colour and I are one. I am a painter.' He meant that he finally understood the meaning of colour and that he could at last be a proper painter. He stored many images in his memory and they came out in his art over many years. He served in World War I, but he did not fight on the Front. He spent much of the time painting aeroplane wings and found plenty of time for his own work. However, he was very upset by the death of his closest friend Marc during the war.

Robert Delaunay 1885–1941

Robert Delaunay was a French painter who developed the movement called Orphism, a branch of Cubism that gave priority to the use of rich, exciting colour. Equally important in its development was his wife, the painter and textile designer Sonia Delaunay-Terk. They explored the links between colour and movement, and their work became very **abstract** by 1912. Marc and Macke had seen Delaunay's 'window' pictures and liked the way the scenes were broken up as if seen through a crystal. Together with Klee and some other Expressionists, they adopted certain aspects of Delaunay's work, introducing fragmented geometric shapes and split planes into their paintings which made them appear more abstract.

In Munich in 1919 a major exhibition of 362 of Klee's paintings made him internationally famous. In 1920 he was invited by the founder of the Bauhaus school of design, Walter Gropius, to teach there. He moved with his family, following the various homes of the Bauhaus until 1930 when he left to teach at the Düsseldorf Art Academy. During his time at the Bauhaus, he became very inspirational as a teacher and writer of theories on art. When the Nazis rose to power and declared all Expressionist art '**degenerate**', Klee campaigned against this idea, which led to his dismissal from the Düsseldorf Academy in 1933. He returned to Berne, depressed by the political situation and his art became darker in both colour and content. He began to suffer from scleroderma, the rare disease that causes hardening of certain areas of the body, such as the skin, heart and lungs, which caused his death in 1940. He continued to paint till the very end.

▮▮▮ *Paul Klee in 1921, not long after he began teaching at the Bauhaus in Berlin.*

Oskar Kokoschka 1886–1980

- Born 1 March 1886 at Pöchlarn on the Danube, in Austria.
- Died 22 February 1980 in Villeneuve near Montreux, Switzerland.

Key works

Murderer, Hope of Women, 1909
Portrait of Herwarth Walden, 1910
The Temptation of Christ, 1911–12
The Tempest or The Bride of the Wind, 1914
'The Emigrés', 1916–17

More than any other artist in this book, Kokoschka stuck to Expressionism throughout his long life. He was a sensitive person who came to painting, despite his training in craft, as a way to communicate his feelings. He suffered from neuralgia (intermittent pain in nerves) and he transferred the constant pain of this onto figures in his paintings by making the nerves visible as scratchy lines. However, his life decisions were driven as much by the need to earn a living as by his emotions.

Oskar Kokoschka was born in 1886 at Pöchlarn in Austria. His father Gustav was a goldsmith from an upper-class family in Prague, Czechoslovakia. His mother Romana was the daughter of an imperial forester in Styria and it was from her that Oskar inherited his love of nature. Oskar was the second son of four children but his older brother had died at an early age. He had wanted to be a research chemist to comply with his father's wishes, but a teacher at the School of Applied Art in Vienna had been impressed by his drawings and recommended him for a scholarship. He started there in 1905, aged nineteen. He intended to be an art teacher. Kokoschka wrote that the curriculum there was about skill in drawing 'leaves and flowers and stems, twisting about like dragons. Drawing the human figure was taboo.' He also learned calligraphy, printmaking and bookbinding, but not painting.

In 1906 he saw a van Gogh exhibition and decided he preferred the intensity of portraits compared to decorative patterns. He set up his own opportunities to paint from the human figure and began employing models. He chose really thin models, especially circus children, so he could see all their joints and muscles. He continued his craft activities because he needed to earn money. From 1907 to 1909 he was a member of the **Weiner Werkstätte**, where he could design tapestries, illustrate books and, most helpfully, exhibit them.

He wrote a play called *Murderer, Hope of Women*, which caused a scandal on its performance in 1909 because of its violence and unstructured style. His poster for the play was so expressive that it was noticed by an architect, Adolf Loos. He said he would provide money and commissions if Kokoschka would leave the Weiner Werkstätte. Loos introduced him to many Viennese intellectuals and artists and he began to paint their portraits. Unfortunately some sitters refused to buy their portraits as they were not very flattering or realistic. They called him a 'soul-ripper' because he seemed to rip away the social mask to expose the soul.

In 1910 he moved to Berlin, which had become an important artistic centre and where Loos had found him work on a magazine called *Der Sturm (The Storm)*. He painted more portraits, which did not make him better off, but did give him a reputation. He also became known for his work on *Der Sturm*, with its editor, Herwarth Walden. Kokoschka said, 'I founded the first German magazine for contemporary art. I was its graphic artist, poet, theatre critic, advertising manager and distributor.' However, despite making a name for himself he was making hardly any money.

▐▌ *The Power of Music*, by Oskar Kokoschka (1918)
The Power of Music *was painted at a time when Kokoschka was beginning to see artistic success, if not financial security.*

Only a year later, tired of his life of poverty and hardship, he returned home to Vienna to earn a steady income as an assistant at the School of Applied Art. He continued to exhibit in Germany and contribute to *Der Sturm*. People in Vienna were not ready for his difficult art and an exhibition there which included his work was badly received by the critics in 1911.

Kokoschka had an affair with Alma Mahler, the widow of the famous composer Gustav Mahler. This was the first time he had been deeply involved with a woman. He travelled to Italy with her in 1913, where he was inspired by the Venetian artists Titian and Tintoretto. This romantic time ended in 1914 when he volunteered to fight in World War I and was seriously wounded a year later. He spent a long time in military hospital recovering from his head wound and lung injury, but he was not affected mentally by the war. In 1917 he moved to Dresden where he carried on painting, but struggled with his injuries, particularly the damage to his ear caused by a bullet passing through his head. It affected his balance for many years. He was also lonely so he had a life-size doll made, which he saw as a friend and a model, painting it over and over again. He was achieving success with his art, however, and was given a professorship at the Dresden Academy of Art from 1919. Although in later years his paintings sold for large sums of money, he never became very wealthy. He continued to give much of what he earned to his family.

From 1923 until his death in 1980 he lived in five different countries. After hearing that he was to be made rector of the Academy of Art and not wishing to take on so much administrative responsibility, he suddenly decided to leave Dresden and the Professorship. He went to Switzerland and then home to Vienna when he heard his father was seriously ill. After his father died, Kokoschka moved to Paris. He made daily visits to the Louvre to see the work of other artists, but did little work himself. He then went on many painting trips round Europe, North Africa and the Middle East, until 1933 when he returned to Vienna. Then a year later he moved to Prague in Czechoslovakia, where his sister was living. Here he met Olda Pavlovska, who later became his wife. In 1938 he had to escape the Nazis having been branded as **degenerate**, so he and Olda emigrated to London as poor refugees. In 1947, he became a British citizen. In 1953 he moved to his final home in Villeneuve, near Lake Geneva, Switzerland. Despite failing eyesight, he continued to paint and draw until he died in 1980, a week before his 94th birthday.

▌▌ *Oskar Kokoschka – the artist in his studio.*

Käthe Kollwitz 1867–1945

- Born on 8 July 1867 in Königsberg, East Prussia, Germany (now in Russia).
- Died 22 April 1945 at Moritzburg Castle, near Dresden, Germany.

Key works

A Weavers' Uprising, series, 1893–7
The Peasants' War, series, 1902–8
Widows and Orphans, 1919
War memorial at Diksmuide, Flanders, 1932 – called 'The Parents' Monument'
Death, series, 1934-5

Käthe Kollwitz had a strong desire to work as an artist, at a time when women were expected only to play at art. She became a well-known artist, partly because of her professionalism and political activity, and partly because her art is deeply moving.

Kollwitz was born in Königsberg in 1867, the third of four children. She had an older brother, Konrad and older sister, Julie. She also had a younger sister, Lise, to whom she was very close. Her parents, Karl and Katherine Schmidt, had strong moral and social beliefs. Her father was a stone mason. Kollwitz said, 'from my childhood on, my father had expressly wished me to be trained for a career as an artist, and he was sure there would be no great obstacles to my becoming one'. She trained under the engraver, Rudolf Mauer from the age of 14.

At the age of seventeen she enrolled at the School for Women Artists in Berlin, as women could rarely enter the main art schools. She was influenced at this time by the work of Max Klinger, particularly his series 'A Life' and also the writings of Emile Zola. It was at this point that she first began to use etchings and lithography to depict social injustices.

In 1891 she married Karl Kollwitz, a doctor who worked in one of the slum districts of Berlin. They were both passionately concerned about the poverty in the slums around them and the injustice of the spread of wealth in Berlin. Kollwitz tried to challenge society's acceptance of this inequality through her art. There were two ways in which she tried to reach a wide public with this message. One was to make prints or posters that could be multiplied and sold cheaply. The other was always to make images of people whose poses and faces expressed strong emotions. Her style was simple, powerful and bold to put her message across as clearly as possible. The pictures which brought her success in 1899 were a series of six prints showing *A Weavers' Uprising*. These were inspired by a play by Hauptmann.

In 1898 she became the first woman to teach at the School for Women Artists. This is a measure of her success, given that few other women taught in art schools. In 1904 she studied sculpture at the Académie Julien, where she met the sculptor Rodin. She won the Villa Romana prize in 1907, which allowed her to travel to Florence, Italy. In 1909 she returned to Germany and contributed illustrations to an art journal called *Simplizissimus*. She became increasingly involved in socialist politics. In 1910, she concentrated on making sculptures for a time.

Just after the start of World War I, her youngest son Peter was killed in action. This was a personal tragedy, but she did not wallow in her grief. It made her even more determined to show how working people were exploited to fight their governments' wars and expand their industries.

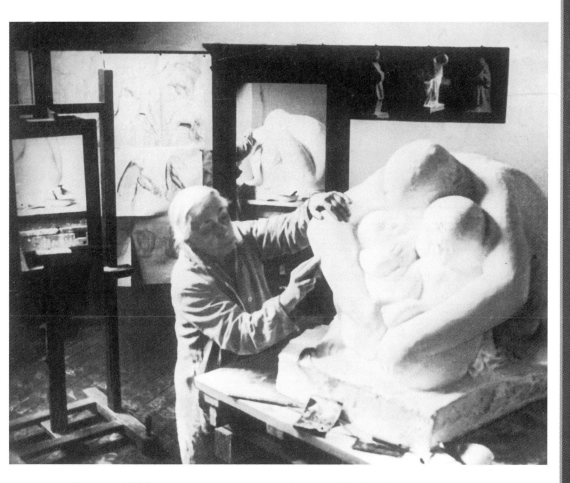

||| *Kollwitz in 1932 – one of the overriding themes of Kollwitz's work is that of the mother and child, as seen here in the sculpture she is working on,* Mother with her Two Children.

She wanted to depict the human suffering and emotion that war caused. She showed the effects of war and loss particularly on women and children, for example in works like *Widows and Orphans* (1919) and *The Survivors* (1923). Other artists, such as Beckmann, Grosz and Dix, were moved to express anti-war feelings in their work, to present a stark, honest, sometimes shocking view of their times. However, more than any other artist of her time Kollwitz was anxious to show the terrible suffering of the postwar years.

Kollwitz was often asked to produce posters for aid organizations in order to increase awareness of the problems Germany was suffering at the time. In 1920 Kollwitz joined Albert Einstein (the famous scientist), George Grosz and others to form the International Workers Aid (IAH), for which she produced posters such as *Help Russia* and *Vienna is Dying! Save her Children!* She said, 'I would like to exert influences in these times when human beings are so perplexed and in need of help', meaning she wanted to guide people to her way of thinking.

In 1926 Kollwitz and her husband visited their son's grave in Belgium. Kollwitz finally completed the memorial figure for Peter in 1931 and it was displayed at the spring exhibition at the Academy in Berlin before being moved to Belgium. The memorial drew much admiration and established Kollwitz as a sculptor as well as a graphic artist.

In the 1920s and early 1930s Kollwitz was a respected and active member of the art world. She was director of master classes for graphic arts and by 1928 she was made the first woman department head at the Prussian Academy of Arts in Berlin. This came to an end when the Nazis rose to power. She had to resign from the Academy because in 1932 she had signed an appeal of unity against the Nazis, bringing to their attention her anti-Nazi feelings. However, because her art was small-scale and could be printed in journals, she could continue to make statements about war and power, for example with a series of eight prints on the theme of *Death* (1934-5).

Her work was not officially labelled **degenerate** but she was banned from exhibiting. Unlike other artists of the time, Kollwitz remained in Berlin during the war despite living and working in the middle of the Allied bombing zone. When World War II came, history repeated itself when her grandson, again named Peter, was killed. Her husband Karl died in 1940. In 1943 her home and studio were bombed and much of her life's work destroyed. She lived in virtual seclusion from 1933 till her death just a few weeks before the war ended in 1945, at Moritzburg Castle near Dresden.

■■ *Women Remembering II*, by Käthe Kollwitz (1920)
*Kollwitz produced many self-portraits throughout her life and this one was
made around the time that she became the first woman to be elected to
the Berlin Academy of Art.*

August Macke 1887–1914

- Born 3 January 1887 in Meschede, Germany.
- Died 26 September 1914 in Champagne, France.

Key works
Zoological Garden I, 1912
Large, Well-lit Shop Window, 1912
Lady in a Green Jacket, 1913
Girls Among Trees, 1914

August Macke was an important member of *Der Blaue Reiter*, and his colourful paintings were well liked. His work is less **abstract** than other *Blaue Reiter* artists, but it might have become more so had he lived longer.

August Macke was born in 1887 in Meschede, Germany. His father, August Friedrich Hermann, was a building engineer and his mother, Florentine, was the daughter of a farmer. He had one older sister called Ottilie. Macke began to draw

August Macke, by Maler (1906)
Macke was one of the most prolific Expressionist artists.

at the age of fifteen and showed early talent. From the age of seventeen, for two years (1904–6), he went to the Academy of Art and the School of Applied Art in Düsseldorf. He designed sets and costumes for the theatre there, using his strong sense of pattern and colour. In the second year he began to make trips abroad to see more art, and in two years he visited Italy, Belgium, Holland and England. This was rounded off with a trip to Paris in June 1907. He had seen Impressionist art in a book, but wanted to see it for real, and he especially liked Manet and Degas. In October 1907 Macke settled again for a year of study at Lovis Corinth's painting school in Berlin, but he could not resist going back to Paris to look at the work of other artists.

In 1909 Macke married Elizabeth Gerhardt, whom he had first met in 1903 on the way to school when she was fifteen. After a honeymoon in Paris, they lived for a year in the country at Tegernsee, near Bonn. In this happy time he painted about 200 pictures. He wrote, 'I'm working fearfully hard now. Working, for me, means celebrating everything simultaneously, nature, sunlight, trees, plants, people, animals, flowers and pots, tables, chairs, mountains, the reflection of water on growing things.'

At the end of that year he made contact with the New Artists' Association in Munich. He had spotted drawings and prints by Marc in the Brackl Gallery. Excited by them, he searched for Marc and they became friends. In April 1910 Macke's son Walter was born and in November of that year the family returned to Bonn. In 1911 he began to contribute to *Der Blaue Reiter* almanac. In 1912 he travelled with Marc to Paris. There they met Robert Delaunay, an artist whom they both admired and who was to become a friend.

In February 1913 Macke's second son Wolfgang was born. Later that year Macke had the idea of going to paint in Tunisia in North Africa. He had been on a painting trip to Lake Thun in Switzerland and he said that he saw the 'world as visual poetry'. He felt that by seeing a place so different from Europe, it would make this poetic vision even more pure. He went to Tunis in 1914 with Paul Klee, whom he had met in Switzerland. They were there for only two weeks but he created 37 beautiful watercolours in that time. Back home these inspired a series of large paintings. However, he had only six weeks before he was called up for military service in World War I. Tragically, he was killed in action in Champagne on 26 September 1914.

▮▮ *Kairouan I*, by August Macke (1914)
Kairouan I *was painted, along with 37 others, while on a two-week holiday in Tunisia with Paul Klee. He also made hundreds of drawings during this time.*

Franz Marc 1880–1916

- Born 8 February 1880 in Munich, Germany.
- Died 4 March 1916 at Verdun in France.

Key works
Blue Horse, 1911
Red Roe Deer II, 1912
Tiger, 1912
The Fate of the Animals, 1913

Franz Marc is known for his animal paintings and for being a key member of *Der Blaue Reiter*. He believed that artists should look into themselves to make art more **spiritual**.

Franz Marc in 1912. Like his friend, August Macke, Marc was killed while fighting in World War I.

At the time of Marc's birth in 1880, his father, Wilhelm Marc, was a professor of painting at the Munich Academy, although he had trained as a lawyer. His mother, Sophie, was from Alsace in France. He had an older brother, Paul. At first Marc had wanted to study religion, but had to put off his studies to do a year of national service. On his return, he decided that he could best develop his spiritual ambitions as a painter, so he studied art with philosophy at the Academy of Fine Art in Munich until 1903. In that year he made his first trips to Paris, where the Impressionists' paintings he saw had a profound effect on him, although his idea that art should look inwards was opposite to their idea of depicting outer appearances.

In 1904 Marc decided to leave the Academy. His first animal drawings appeared in 1905. He struggled with his paintings, often destroying them, especially any pictures of people. In 1907 he began making studies of animal anatomy at Berlin Zoo, trying to commit it to memory so that he did not have to paint animals from life but could look inwards and paint them from his imagination. For three years from 1907 he taught anatomy in his studio. He had made an unhappy and short-lived marriage to fellow student Marie Schnür in 1906. However, he formed a much happier relationship with Maria Francke a year later and married her in 1908.

In 1910 Marc had his first exhibition, at the Munich gallery of a dealer called Brackl. The critics liked it and artists such as Macke made contact with him. They became friends. A relative of Macke's helped Marc, who was struggling financially, by regularly buying paintings from him. In 1911, in collaboration with Kandinsky, von Jawlensky and Macke, Marc began working on *Der Blaue Reiter*.

An important event for him was a visit with Macke to France in 1912 to meet Robert Delaunay, whose ideas about movement fascinated him. On the other hand, the artist he least agreed with was Max Beckmann. They had an ongoing argument in magazine articles, in which Beckmann said that good art was the skilful painting of appearances, but Marc said it was 'inner greatness', the expression of feelings inspired by looking at something.

In 1914 he volunteered for military service in World War I, believing that war might sweep away the old social and cultural forces and bring in new ones, but he was never to find out if he was right. He was killed on 4 March 1916 at Verdun. An exhibition in his memory at the Sturm Gallery in Berlin showed him to be an important artist.

Blue Horse I, by Franz Marc (1911) *Marc was best-known for his animal drawings and painted many pictures of horses at this time. Blue Horse I had an almost magical quality because of the bold, unrealistic colours.*

Paula Modersohn-Becker 1876–1907

- Born 8 February 1876 in Dresden, Germany.
- Died 20 November 1907 in Worpswede, Germany.

Key works

Self-portrait with Amber Necklace, 1906
Nude Girl with Goldfish Bowl, 1906
Still-life with Sunflowers, 1907

Paula Modersohn-Becker sold only three paintings and was hardly known in her lifetime, but now her work is seen as very important. Within her circle, she broke many rules of the time about what art should be. She painted herself nude for example. She made paintings with a formal strength that set her apart from other artists of her time. Her life is a classic story of a woman torn between a husband and a desire for independence in her work.

Born in February 1876 in Dresden, Germany, Paula Becker was the third child of respectable parents. She was determined to train as an artist but her father at first refused, so from 1893 she spent two years training to be a teacher. However, in 1896 she persuaded her father to support her financially when she was accepted to study drawing and painting at the Society of Women Artists in Berlin.

Self-portrait with Camelia branch, by Paula Modersohn-Becker (1907)
Probably the most important female artist of her day, Modersohn-Becker produced 750 paintings in her short career.

In 1897 Becker met her future husband, the landscape painter Otto Modersohn, while living in an artists' colony in Worpswede, near Berlin. The colony was set up in 1884 by Fritz Mackensen. Several artists lived and worked together, learning from Mackensen in an informal way. The colony was set in bleak but beautiful moorland and their painting aimed to capture this wildness and the simplicity of rural life.

However peaceful she found Worpswede, she wanted to learn from other people besides Mackensen, so in January 1900 she went to study in Paris. She had an exciting time and met the artist Emil Nolde. After returning to Worpswede later in the year she became friendly with the poet Rainer Maria Rilke. On the 25 May 1901 she married Otto Modersohn. The marriage gave her financial security to continue painting, but she was not entirely at one with the other artists in the colony, including her husband. They could not leave behind depth and the rules of perspective as she had. Otto said her style was crude. In his diary of 1903 he wrote, 'Paula hates all conventions, and she has now fallen for the mistake of making everything angular, ugly, bizarre and wooden. The colours are great – but the forms! The style! Hands like spoons, noses like conkers, mouths like gashes, faces like imbeciles. She's attempting too much ... She won't listen to advice as usual.'

These simple forms did not come from a childish lack of skill, however, but from careful research of classical Greek, Egyptian and Roman art. Her subject matter was not invented or fanciful, but included self-portraits and local rural people, especially women and children.

From 1903 to 1906 she made three long trips to Paris, where like Kollwitz in 1904 she met the sculptor Rodin and studied at the Académie Julien. This time she was impressed by the **Nabis** artists as well as van Gogh and Cézanne. This interest in Cézanne shows that she cared most about making good, solid paintings and less about making expressive, dramatic scenes.

During 1906–07 Modersohn-Becker remained in Paris for a year, intending to leave her husband for good and devote herself to the challenge of painting. However, he went to Paris and they spent the winter there together. In the spring he persuaded her to return to Worpswede with him – she was pregnant. She was clearly very happy to have a baby girl, Mathilde, in November 1907. Sadly, she died from an embolism (obstruction to an artery) soon after the birth.

Edvard Munch 1863–1944

- Born on 12 December 1863 on a farm at Engelhaug near Loten in southern Norway.
- Died of pneumonia 23 January 1944 in Oslo, Norway.

Key works
Death in the Sick Chamber, 1892
The Scream, 1893
By the Deathbed, 1895
Virginia Creeper, 1898
The Sick Child, 1907

Munch is the most important modern Norwegian painter, and a major influence on *Die Brücke* artists. He did not call himself an Expressionist, but his pictures express moods very strongly, especially sadness and grief. He wrote: 'For as long as I can remember I have suffered from a deep feeling of anxiety which I have tried to express in my art.'

Soon after Munch's birth in 1863, the family moved to Christiania, now called Oslo. His was a distinguished family. On his father's side there were high-ranking churchmen and his uncle Peter was one of Norway's great historians. His father, Christian, was a military doctor. His mother, Laura, came from a well-to-do farming family. Edvard was the second of five children. Most of what is known about Munch's life comes from his journals and letters written to his sister Inger and to his Aunt Karen, who looked after the family after his mother died from tuberculosis in 1868 when he was five. She was a warm, affectionate mother substitute who encouraged the boy's artistic ability. Her letters to him show her to have been a wise and sympathetic friend through the worst times of his life. Munch's father had been so badly affected by his wife's death that he took to an extreme form of **religious fervour**. Munch wrote of how his father could be playful one moment, then suddenly violent, giving frenzied punishments. He wrote: 'In my childhood I felt that I was always treated unjustly, without a mother, sick, and with threatened punishment in Hell hanging over my head.' This shows that he was deeply affected first by the physical illness of his mother and then by the mental distress of his father, which caused his father to behave so irrationally.

However, there were some brighter moments. Munch enjoyed going with his doctor father to visit his patients in hospital, where he could draw them in bed and learn how to compose small groups of figures.

■ *Munch's life was one of great sadness and grief and it is these emotions that can be traced through many of his paintings.*

Sickness was to become a frequent theme in his work. Not only had he to cope with his own bouts of ill-health, suffering from asthmatic bronchitus and several severe attacks of rheumatic fever, which badly interrupted his schooling, but in 1879, when he was fourteen, his older sister Sophie died from the same disease as their mother. Tuberculosis was a slow, painful condition. It must have greatly affected the sensitive boy to watch while another loved one wasted away. Eight years later Munch began to paint the first of six versions of that scene, called *The Sick Child*. This picture seems quite conventional to us today but it caused an outrage when it was first exhibited at the Oslo Autumn Exhibition in 1886 because it was totally unlike anything that had came before it.

Aged seventeen, Munch began to study art formally when his father, having given up hope of him becoming an engineer, allowed him to enter the Oslo State School of Art and Handcraft. The following year (1881) he produced his first significant painting, *The Hospital Ward*, and then followed several portraits and family studies. During the next twenty years he travelled extensively in France, Italy and Germany. In Paris in 1885 he came under the influence of the Impressionists and from 1890 it was first the **Nabis** and then the Post-Impressionists, especially van Gogh and Gauguin, who claimed his attention.

All the time the emotional intensity of Munch's own work anticipated that of the Expressionists. During the 1890s he began working on a large series of paintings he called *The Frieze of Life* ('a poem of life, love and death'). In 1892 he took 55 pictures to Berlin for an exhibition. They included some of the major *Frieze of Life* paintings and *The Sick Child*. His work caused such an uproar that the exhibition was closed after one week mainly because of the uncompromising personal subject-matter. Although the art establishment also criticized his technical ability saying his portraits were 'so sloppily daubed that at times it is difficult to identify them as human figures ... they are an insult to art'. The younger artists of Berlin were angry at Munch's treatment and formed themselves into a group called the Berlin **Secession**. Munch remained in Berlin, finding many important friends and gradually he gained general support for his work. In 1902 he exhibited 22 of his *Frieze* paintings, many of which he also produced as woodcuts and etchings, for example *The Kiss* and *The Scream*. These made a great impact, as the emotion could be seen in the wild gestures of the marks as well as in the subject matter.

Munch never married and he always found relationships with women difficult. In 1908, after the painful end of a love affair, combined with overwork and too much alcohol, he suffered a mental breakdown while travelling home to Norway. He spent eight months in hospital in Copenhagen, Denmark. He wrote, 'I would not cast off my illness for there is much in my art that I owe to it.' For a while his pictures became more extrovert and his colours became brighter. In 1914, back in Norway, he was commissioned to paint a series of large murals for the University Hall of Oslo, depicting the forces of nature, science and history. He completed these in 1916. Later, as he struggled with illness and self-doubt, his work became once more anguished, tortured and full of emotion. After his breakdown he never left Norway. In 1916 he settled in Ekely, Oslo, and lived a solitary life. His 70th birthday in 1933 was internationally recognized, but his works were considered '**degenerate**' by the Nazis and removed from German museums. He died peacefully of pneumonia at the age of 80 in 1944, two years after his first exhibition in the USA.

Virginia Creeper, by Edvard Munch (1898)
Regarded as a pioneer in the Expressionist movement, it is Munch's paintings from the 1890s that the public are most familiar with. Munch's work was exhibited 106 times between the years 1892 and 1909.

Emil Nolde 1867–1956

- Born 7 August 1867 in the tiny hamlet of Nolde, in Schleswig, the northern spit of land near Denmark, now part of Germany.
- Died 16 April 1956 in Seebüll, Schleswig.

Key works

Child and Big Bird, 1912
Life of Christ, 1911–12
Devil and Scholar, 1919
In the Lemon Garden, 1920
Dancers, 1920

There were two important influences in Nolde's artistic life. One was the flat, lonely landscape threatened by the sea, that made him feel the power of nature. In his imagination, the cries of birds and animals became colours and natural forms became strange creatures. The other influence was the strict religious upbringing which never left him. He said: 'When I was a child ... I made a solemn promise to God that when I grew up I would write a hymn ... The vow has never been fulfilled. But I have painted a large number of pictures ... I wonder if they will do instead?'

Born Emile Hansen on 7 August 1867, he took the name of his birthplace, Nolde, in 1901. His parents were farmers and he had three brothers. Nine generations of his family had eked out a living on the family farm. Not cut out for the farming life of his family, during the late 1880s Nolde became an apprentice woodcarver. This took him to Karlsruhe, where he also attended the local School of Arts and Crafts, then to Berlin, where he drew in the museum and became fascinated by Egyptian art.

Then in 1892, when he was 25, he went to St Gallen in Switzerland, to teach ornamental drawing. Until then he knew nothing of contemporary art, but here he discovered the Swiss artists Arnold Böcklin and Ferdinand Hodler. He often walked in the mountains to try to capture the feeling he had seen in their work. He painted the highest peaks, imagining faces on them where light and shadow fell. He turned these drawings into a series of postcards which sold so well that he gave up teaching in 1896 to paint full time.

There followed five years of travel and study – to Dachau (near Munich); to Paris where he saw the Impressionists and studied at the Académie Julien; to Copenhagen, where he met and married Ada Vilstrup, a Danish actress.

■■ *Religion and the natural landscape were major influences upon Nolde.*
He always regretted the fact that none of his paintings were ever on
display in a church.

In 1901 Nolde moved to Berlin with his new wife. Through Ada he was able to draw theatre and cabaret scenes. In 1903 they settled on the island of Alsen, where in summer they lived in a fisherman's hut, and he painted gardens and seascapes in vivid colours. In the winter they returned to Berlin. At the age of 38, he exhibited his work at a one-man show in Dresden. Some members of *Die Brücke* were excited by Nolde's 'tempests of colour' and invited him to join in 1906, which he did for eighteen months. By 1908 he had become quite well known as an artist.

Nolde felt that *Die Brücke* had not become the alliance of new artists that he had hoped for so chose to leave. In 1909 he attempted to form a new group to include such artists as Matisse, Beckmann and Munch, but this failed. He joined the Berlin **Secession** instead. Also in 1909 after suffering a period of severe illness, Nolde began to paint pictures with a strong religious theme but often featuring grotesque imagery. These pictures were controversial however, and it was the rejection by the Berlin Secession of *Pentecost* in 1910 that caused Nolde to bitterly attack the Secession and be expelled as a result. So with other *Brücke* artists, such as Max Pechstein, he helped to found the New Secession.

In Berlin Nolde spent much time in the Museum of Anthropology and began to write a book entitled *Artistic Expression Among Primitive Tribes*. In 1913 he and Ada were invited to join a scientific expedition to New Guinea, and they journeyed there through Russia, Korea, China, Japan and the Palau Islands. In common with other Expressionist artists, Nolde was fascinated by African art and other **primitive** art styles with their bold patterns and contrasting colours, and he was horrified yet thrilled by the idea of head-hunting and cannibalism. He sketched constantly throughout the trip. He described how, just in case of trouble, Ada held a gun over him while he painted the people. He also painted large-scale works at this time but many of these were taken by the British at the start of World War I and not returned to him until many years later.

The early 1920s were spent in more travel around Europe, but in 1926 Nolde bought a farm in Seebüll, near his birthplace. In 1937 he built a grand modern house with a large gallery on the farm. However, in the same year, a thousand of his pictures were taken by the Nazis from museums. He was devastated to be branded a **degenerate** as he considered himself a good German and was a member of the Nazi party. In 1941 the **Gestapo** raided his house and took away everything that enabled him to make art. Until 1945, however, he managed secretly, and at the risk of imprisonment if he was found out, to make over 1300 small watercolours, named later *Unpainted Pictures*. A further blow to Nolde was the bombing of his Berlin studio, from which only a bundle of charred drawings was saved. He lived at Seebüll until his death at the age of 89. The house is now the Nolde Museum.

■■■ *The Sea III*, by Emil Nolde (1913)

*Nolde's first biographer, Max Sauerlandt, described Nolde's love of the sea:
'Nolde understands the sea like no other painter before him. He sees it not
from the beach or from a boat but as it exists in itself eternally in motion,
ever changing...'*

Max Pechstein 1881–1955

- Born 31 December 1881 in Eckersbach, near Zwickau, an industrial part of Germany.
- Died 29 June 1955 in Berlin, Germany.

Key works
Horse Fair, 1910
Before the Storm, 1910
Summer in the Dunes, 1911
Palau Islands triptych, 1917

Max Pechstein was the first *Die Brücke* member to become popular – his paintings were not as shocking as those of the other artists. He won an award for painting, the State Prize of Saxony in 1907 and at the time was seen as the leading figure of German Expressionism. However, he is now seen as a minor figure. He differed from the others in that he was the only one with a formal training in the 'craft' of painting, and he was from a poorer background so was perhaps more driven to achieve popular success.

The success achieved by Pechstein in his early career was a cause of jealousy with Ernst Kirchner, another member of Die Brucke.

Pechstein's father was a textile worker. Pechstein began taking drawing lessons at the age of 15 and then from 1896 to 1900 was apprenticed to a decorative painter in Zwickau. Then for two years he studied at the Dresden School of Applied Art, where he won many prizes. He was invited to be a teacher there, but he had ambitions to be a fine artist so he decided to study at the Academy of Fine Arts in Dresden (1902–6). In 1906 Pechstein joined *Die Brücke* after meeting Erich Heckel. He had been angry because workers installing a mural of his had toned down a red tulip field with grey. Heckel had appeared at his side and shouted in his support.

In 1907, Pechstein won a scholarship from the Dresden Academy that allowed him to travel to Italy for the first time. He also went to France to see the Fauvists. He then moved to Berlin to be in the heart of the established art world. He was busy there, becoming a member of the Berlin **Secession** and exhibiting with them in 1909, with some success. In 1910, Pechstein's work and that of 26 other artists was refused by the Secession. He helped to found the New Secession, which included the *Brücke* members and *Blaue Reiter* painters.

A year later he set up an art school called the MUIM Institute, with Ernst Kirchner. He also got married and spent his honeymoon in Italy. All this time he was still a member of *Die Brücke*, most of whom by 1912 had moved to Berlin. The other members had made a pact to have nothing to do with the more traditional Berlin Secession, so when Pechstein exhibited with the Secession without their consent, they asked him to leave *Die Brücke*.

In the Dresden Ethnological Museum, Kirchner had discovered the carvings of the Palau Islanders. Pechstein liked them too and he wanted to experience such a culture for himself, so in 1914 he travelled with his wife to the Palau Islands in Micronesia. Pechstein's time in paradise ended too soon when World War I broke out. He was captured by the Japanese, sent back to Germany (via the USA, where his wife remained) and drafted into the army. As with many artists who survived their military service, he suffered a mental breakdown.

However, he recovered and became a member of the prestigious Prussian Academy of Arts. However, in 1933 he and others were forbidden to paint or exhibit by the Nazis and he was later branded as **degenerate**. In 1944 his Berlin flat was bombed, destroying many of his paintings. After World War II was over he was able to work and teach freely again, and was a professor in Berlin up until his death in 1955.

Red Houses, by Max Pechstein (1923)

Pechstein was considered the most important Expresssionist at one time, but he never thought that way about himself. He simply felt, 'art has been and remains the part of my life that brings me happiness.'

Egon Schiele 1890–1918

- Born on 12 June 1890 in Tulln, a small town in Austria.
- Died 31 October 1918 in Vienna, Austria.

Key works

Grimacing Man (Self-Portrait), 1910
Self-portrait with Black Clay Vase and Spread Fingers, 1911
Self-portrait with Head Lowered, 1912
Self-portrait with Chinese Lantern Plant, 1912

Schiele is now the most well-known Austrian Expressionist, although at first his art was too disturbing to be widely accepted. He was born in Tulln, Austria, where his father Adolf was the railway station master. Of six siblings, only three survived. He always felt himself to be different and at school in Tulln, then in Krems, he spent all his spare time drawing. His mother said that he began to draw at eighteen months old, so in a family with no artistic tradition he was a prodigy.

In 1902 the family moved to Klosterneuberg and Schiele went to the prestigious Abbey School, where he did badly at everything except art. He felt the teachers did not understand him. The death of his father, sent insane by a long illness, put more strain on the fourteen-year-old boy. However, things improved when a new art teacher, Ludwig Strauch, encouraged him and he produced some very accomplished drawings. Schiele's new guardian Uncle Leopold was annoyed by the boy's poor academic performance but Strauch persuaded him to let Schiele study at the Vienna Academy of Art.

At that time the artist Gustav Klimt (1862–1918) had a considerable influence on young artists in Vienna, and when Schiele met him in 1907 he asked his opinion on a folder of drawings. Klimt was very impressed and the two became lifelong friends. Schiele began to copy Klimt's style, with bold lines and silver and gold paint. He had his first exhibition in Klosterneuberg, and then a more important one in Vienna in 1909, the same year that he left the Academy. Two of the works, portraits of his friends Hans Massman and Anton Peschka (who married his sister Gerti) clearly show Klimt's influence. Some of the artists who exhibited formed themselves into the New Art Group. Schiele was the founder of the group.

Schiele continued to exhibit with and without the New Art Group throughout Austria and Germany. From 1910 he developed his own style and his work drew mixed reactions. In 1911 he exhibited with the *Der Blaue Reiter* artists. While recognizing his talent, some people were disturbed by his stretched, skeletal figures and grimacing faces.

Schiele lived an unsettled life, often in poverty. He travelled to his mother's birthplace in Bohemia, then back to Austria, trying to gain the appreciation he felt he deserved. Finally in 1912 he found a studio and apartment in Vienna. Here in 1914 he met Edith Harms, whom he married in 1915 just days before he was called up for military service. After training in Bohemia, accompanied by his wife, he returned to Vienna where he was given guard duties and clerical work. He was allowed to keep on painting and exhibiting. The year 1917–18 was a time of great productivity and success. He sold many of the 50 pictures he showed with the Vienna **Secession**. He exhibited in many cities and was praised by critics. Almost all his work was bought by collectors and his talents were finally recognized.

One sadness for Schiele in February 1918 was the death of Klimt after a stroke. Schiele was with him when he died. In October an influenza epidemic swept through Europe, killing millions of war-weakened, starving people. It took first Edith, who was expecting their baby, and three days later Schiele, aged only 28.

Self-portrait with Black Clay Vase and Spread Fingers, by Egon Schiele (1911)
From 1910–11, Schiele developed his own style and his colours became stronger and brighter.

The Next Generation

Expressionism as a movement died off in the early 1920s, although many of the artists continued to be successful. It was partly killed by its own success, because younger artists (for example, **Dadaists**) saw it as too staid, whereas **conservative** thinkers and politicians saw it as **decadent**. When Hitler accused the Expressionists of being **degenerate** and stripped German museums of their paintings, many emigrated to America or France where their art and teaching influenced younger artists.

Kandinsky and Klee were influential as teachers at the Bauhaus in the 1920s and 30s and their interest in form rather than content contributed to trends in the art world until at least the 1960s. Most Bauhaus students became designers and architects, but with a clear awareness of the **aesthetic** values of fine art, which meant that their designs were not only functional but also pleasing to look at.

The legacy of Expressionism
USA

Expressionism had a big impact in the USA, especially in New York, as European artists emigrated there. Max Beckmann and George Grosz, as well as another European, Arshile Gorky, were influential through their teaching in

Alchemy, by Jackson Pollock (1947)
Pollock's style of painting was very similar to that of other Expressionist artists in that he felt the art came from within: 'today painters do not have to go to a subject-matter outside themselves'.

New York in the 1940s. However, Expressionism was not just a European import in the USA, but a **cross-fertilization** between American and various European movements. This was one of the influences on the rich variety of styles covered by the term Abstract Expressionism, which would come to dominate the western art world in the 1950s. Mark Rothko (1903–70), Barnett Newman (1905–70) and Clyfford Still (1904–80) shared Beckmann's interest in large-scale, serious paintings, but like Kandinsky and Klee they wanted colour or marks to communicate the meanings, rather than people and symbolic objects. Rothko, Newman and Helen Frankenthaler developed a type of painting filled with flat colours, called 'colour field', which can be linked to the **spiritual** importance of colour explored by Kandinsky and Klee.

Britain

From 1935 to 1955 the **Neo-Romantic** painters, such as Graham Sutherland, John Piper and Cecil Collins, shared the Expressionists' nostalgic view of nature. Also, as in America, Britain produced **abstract** painters who had picked up Expressionist ideas, including Ben Nicholson, Peter Lanyon and Patrick Heron, all based in St Ives in Cornwall. In general, although expressive, the subject matter of mid-20th-century British art was not disturbing, with one notable exception – Francis Bacon.

Timeline

1860   James Ensor born on 13 April

1863   Edvard Munch born on 12 December

1866   Wassily Kandinsky born on 4 December

1867   Käthe Kollwitz born 8 July

       Emil Nolde born 7 August

1876   Paula Modersohn-Becker born 8 February

1879   Paul Klee born on 18 December

1880   Ernst Ludwig Kirchner born 6 May

       Franz Marc born 8 February

1881   Max Pechstein born 31 December

1884   Max Beckmann born on 12 February

1886   Oskar Kokoschka born on 1 March

1887   August Macke born on 3 January

1890   Egon Schiele born on 12 June

1903   **Weiner Werkstätte** set up in Vienna

1905	**Fauvism** exhibition at the **Salon** d'Automne
	Die Brücke (The Bridge) group is formed by Kirchner, Heckel, Schmidt-Rottluff and Bleyl
1909	The Berlin **Secession** formed
1911	Kandinsky and Marc form Der Blaue Reiter
1913	Die Brücke breaks up
1914	World War I begins
1917	Russian Revolution begins
1918	World War I ends
1919	Bauhaus school of art and design is opened
1920	First International **Dada** Fair
1928	Kollwitz made first woman department head at the Prussian Academy of Arts in Berlin
1933	Hitler comes to power in Germany
	The Bauhaus is closed by the Nazis
1937	The '**Degenerate** Art' exhibition
1939–45	World War II

Glossary

abstract   describes a picture with no recognizable subject, but which is a composition of shape, colour and line

aesthetic   to do with beauty and the appreciation of beautiful things

applied art   art skills applied to useful activities such as interior decoration, architecture, furniture design or commercial graphics. Since the Renaissance it has been considered to be of a lower status than fine art.

avant-garde   art which is forward-looking and experimental

bohemian   describes someone who has rejected the conventional values of society, lives very informally and dresses in an elaborate and decorative way

conservative   describes someone who conforms to strict social rules, is wary of change and holds cautious, moderate views

cross-fertilization   in art, the interchange of ideas that helps in the spread of a movement or style, for example

Dada   'anti-art' art movement, which took place mainly in Zurich and Berlin from 1916. It tried to break down the traditional barriers between art forms. Dada art did not have to make sense. It was very influential on Surrealism.

decadent   lacking in morals; someone who just wants to have fun rather than work hard for the establishment society. The German Weimar governments in the 1920s created a climate in which the arts could flourish. However, the Nazis squashed all this from 1933 onwards.

degenerate   the Nazis wanted to breed a pure, superior race by destroying anything degenerate, which referred to people and ideas that fell outside their narrow vision. They attacked modern art as 'political and cultural anarchy'.

Fauvism   Expressionist style of painting inspired by the Neo-Impressionists and Cézanne, based on intense and vivid colours. It emerged as the first major avant-garde development of the 20th century. The name, meaning 'wild beasts', was coined by a hostile critic in 1905.

German occupation   period of time during World War II when Germany conquered and occupied various European countries

Gestapo   German secret police under the Nazis

history painter   type of artist who told stories in their work from the Bible or from classical mythology. History painting had the highest status of all the genres (types of subject matter), compared to still life and landscape painting, because it was intellectual and was intended for display in the most public and grand places. Max Beckmann wanted to create a modern form of this genre.

Jugendstil   German term for Art Nouveau. It was a movement for decorative art and craft and a reaction against history painting.

manifesto   public statement of the policy or aims of a group or society

modernism   international artistic movement that took place around the time of World War I. Modernist artists believed that the traditional order of things had broken down and there was no existing style that could portray the new reality. They therefore looked for new ways to show this in their art.

Nabis from a Hebrew word meaning 'prophets', the Nabis were a group of artists formed in 1892 by members of the Académie Julien, Paris, who were influenced by Gauguin. Members included Bonnard, Vuillard and Denis.

Neo-Romanticism British movement in painting of 1935–55. 'Neo' means 'new'. Romanticism was a 19th-century movement, which looked beyond surface appearances to the spiritual in nature. The Neo-Romantics brought back a romantic view of the British landscape, at a time when the country was under threat from Nazi invasion.

New Objectivity movement in German painting in the 1920s and early 1930s against abstraction and the fragmentation of Cubism. The artists involved, such as Grosz, Dix and Beckmann, thought that art should be more understandable and realistic, less personal and more political, than Expressionism.

objectivity opposite of subjectivity. If you look at things subjectively you colour them with your own tastes or feelings. If you are objective, you try to see things without any individual prejudice.

parody exaggerated and humorous imitation of, for example, a work of literature or art, or a style

primitive describes a people or a style that is undeveloped and simple

religious fervour passionate, often extreme and obsessive form of devotion to God

Salon French word for 'drawing room'. It came to refer to a major annual exhibition, in which the members of an art academy showed their latest works. It originated in Paris. When the Impressionists were rejected from the Salons, they opened their independent Salon des Refusés.

secession a splitting off from an organization to form a new group. After 1890, in Munich, Berlin and Vienna there were a number of secessions formed from the traditional art academies. Younger artists were reacting against art that glorified royalty and establishment society.

spiritual to do with the soul or spirit of a person rather than the body. Can be used to refer to religious or holy things.

triptych painting or relief carving made on three panels, which are hinged together vertically. Used loosely, it can refer to a set of three paintings.

Twenty Group (Les Vingt) society of artists founded in Brussels, Belgium, by Octave Maus. It supported Symbolist and Neo-Impressionist art in particular. James Ensor was among the first to exhibit with them in 1884.

Weiner Werkstätte (Viennese Workshops) organization of craftspeople and designers set up in Vienna in 1903 to further the ideas and teachings of the great English designer William Morris

Resources

List of famous works

Max Beckmann (1884–1950)
Carnival, 1920, Tate Gallery, London
Self-portrait with Stiff Hat, etching, 1921, Minneapolis Institute of Arts, Minnesota
The Snake Woman, 1921, Art Gallery of New South Wales, Australia
Beach, 1922, Tate Gallery, London

James Ensor (1860–1949)
The Entry of Christ into Brussels, 1888, J. Paul Getty Museum, Los Angeles
Skeletons Warming Themselves, 1889, Kimbell Art Museum, Fort Worth, Texas
Still-life with Flowers and Masks, c. 1928, Stedelijk Museum of Modern Art, Amsterdam
Effect of Light, 1935, Tate Gallery, London

Wassily Kandinsky (1866–1944)
Blue Mountain, 1908–09, Guggenheim Museum, New York
Cossacks, 1910–11, Tate Gallery, London
Improvisation 30 (Cannons), 1913, Art Institute of Chicago
Angle Rouge, 1928, Musée Maillol, France

Ernst Ludwig Kirchner (1880–1938)
Artillerymen, 1915, Guggenheim Museum, New York
Portrait of Ludwig Schames, 1918, Art Gallery of New South Wales
Dresden: Schlossplatz, 1926, The Minneapolis Institute of Arts

Paul Klee (1879–1940)
They're Biting, 1920, Tate Gallery, London
Runner at the Goal, 1921, Guggenheim, New York
Red Balloon, 1922, Guggenheim, New York
New Harmony, 1936, Guggenheim, New York

Oskar Kokoschka (1886–1980)
Murderer, Hope of Women, 1910, Los Angeles County Museum of Art
Portrait of Herwarth Walden, 1910, Staadtsgalerie, Stuttgart
Polperro II, 1939, Tate Gallery, London

Käthe Kollwitz (1867–1945)
Memorial to Karl Liebknecht, 1919–20, Käthe Kollwitz Museum, Berlin
Woman Remembering II, 1920, Fine Arts Museums of San Francisco
Self-portrait, 1921, National Museum of Women in the Arts
War, 1922–23, woodcut series, Käthe Kollwitz Museum, Berlin

Auguste Macke (1887–1914)
Russisches Ballett I, 1912, Kunsthalle Bremen, Germany
Kinder im Garten, 1912, Kunstmuseum, Berlin
Seiltänzer, 1914, Kunstmuseum, Berlin
Türkisches Café I, 1914, Kunstmuseum, Berlin

Franz Marc (1880–1916)
Siberian Dogs in the Snow, 1909–10, National Gallery of Art, Washington
Yellow Cow, 1911, Guggenheim Collection, New York
Blue Horse II, 1911, Fine Arts Museum Bern
Lizards, 1912, Fine Arts Museums of San Francisco

Paula Modersohn-Becker (1876–1907)
Portrait of a Woman, 1898, National Gallery of Art, Washington, USA
Sitting Old Woman, c. 1906, Fine Arts Museums of San Francisco, USA

Edvard Munch (1863–1944)
The Scream, 1893, National Gallery, Oslo
Summer Night in Aasgarstrand, 1904, Musée d'Orsay, Paris
The Sick Child, 1907, Tate Gallery, London

Emil Nolde (1867–1956)
Dance II, 1911, oil-painting, Nolde Museum, Neukirchen, Germany
The Sea B, 1930, Tate Gallery, London
Narcissi and Hyacinths, 1950, San Diego Museum of Art

Max Pechstein (1881–1955)
Beach at Nidden, 1911, Staatliche Museen zu Berlin
After the Bath, c. 1920, The University of Michigan Museum of Art

Egon Schiele (1890–1918)
Seated Woman, Back View, 1917, Metropolitan Museum of Art, New York
Portrait of Paris von Gütersloh, 1918, The Minneapolis Institute of Arts
Dr. Koller, c. 1918, charcoal on japan paper, National Gallery of Art,
Washington DC

Useful websites

Tate Britain, London
www.tate.org.uk

Leopold Museum, Vienna
www.leopoldmuseum.org

National Gallery of Australia, Canberra
www.nga.gov.au

Solomon R. Guggenheim Museum, New York
www.guggenheim.org/new_york_index.html

The Minneapolis Institute of Arts
www.artsmia.org

Further reading

General

Art in Vienna 1898–1918, Peter Vergo, Phaidon, 1975

The Expressionists, Wolf Dieter-Dube, Thames & Hudson, 1972 (republished 1996)

Expressionism, John Willett, London & New York, 1970

Expressionism, Dietmar Elger, Taschen, 1998

German Art in the Twentieth Century, edited by C. Joachimedes, N. Rosenthal & W. Schmied, Royal Academy of Art, London, 1985

The History of Art, Claudio Merle, Hodder Wayland

The History of Western Painting, Juliet Heslewood, Belitha Press

The History of Western Sculpture, Juliet Heslewood, Belitha Press

Movements in Modern Art: Expressionism, Shulamith Behr, 1999, Tate Gallery publishing

20th Century Art: 1900-10 New Ways of Seeing, Jackie Gaff, 2000, Heinemann Library

20th Century Art: 1910-20 Birth of Abstract Art, Jackie Gaff, 2000, Heinemann Library

Understanding Modern Art, M Bohm-Duchen and J Cook, Usborne Publishing

The artists

Max Beckmann, Friedhelm Wilhelm Fischer, (trans. P.S. Falla), Phaidon, London, 1973

Otto Dix 1891–1969, Exhibition catalogue, Tate Gallery, London, 1992

James Ensor: The Creative Years, Diane Lesko, Princeton University Press, New Jersey, 1985

George Grosz, Hans Hess, Yale University Press, New Haven, London, 1985

Ferdinand Hodler, Sharon L. Hirsch, Thames and Hudson, London, 1982

Kandinsky, Francois Le Target, Poligrafa, Barcelona, 1986

1931–1984 Ernst Ludwig Kirchner, Donald E. Gordon, Harvard University Press Cambridge (Mass), 1968

Paul Klee, Carolyn Lanchner, Museum of Modern Art New York, 1987

Oskar Kokoschka 1886–1980, Exhibition catalogue, Tate Gallery, London, 1986

Käthe Kollwitz, Elizabeth Prelinger, with essays by Alessandra Comini and Hildegard Bachert, Washington National Gallery of Art, Yale University Press, New Haven & London, 1992

August Macke 1887–1914, Anna Meseure, Taschen, Cologne, 1993

Franz Marc, Mark Rosenthal, Priestel, Munich, 1989

Paula Modersohn-Becker: Her Life and Work, Gillian Perry, Women's Press, London, 1979

Edvard Munch: The Man and the Artist, Ragna Stang, Gordon Fraser Gallery, London, 1979

Max Pechstein, Magdalena M Moeller, Hirmer Verlag, Germany, 1996

Egon Schiele, Erwin Mitsch, Phaidon Press, London, 1993

Egon Schiele: Eros and Passion, Klaus Albrecht Schroder, Pegasus Library, Prestel, 1999

Index

Titles in the *Artists in Profile* series include:

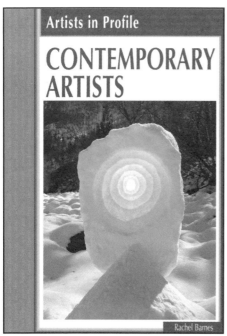

Hardback   0 431 11653 9

Hardback   0 431 11643 1

Hardback   0 431 11640 7

Hardback   0 431 11651 2

Find out about the other titles in this series on our website www.heinemann.co.uk/library